The Art of R Programming

A research based book: Integrating Practical Applications with Foundational Theory in R Programming

—By Eman Ahmad

Table of Contents

1. **Introduction to R**
   - Why R?
   - What is R?
2. **Packages Installation in R**
   - Installing Packages
   - Example Code
3. **The Basics of R**
   - Objects
   - Variables
   - Functions
   - Pre-built Objects
4. **Rules for Naming Variables**
   - Naming Conventions
   - Commenting Your Code
5. **Data Types in R**
   - Overview of Data Types
   - Data Frames
6. **Examining an Object in R**
   - Use of Accessor $
   - Class Function
7. **Factors, Lists, and Matrices in R**
   - Understanding Factors
   - Working with Lists
   - Introduction to Matrices
8. **Vectors in R**
   - Creating Vectors
   - Naming Vectors
   - The Sequence Function
9. **Subsetting, Coercion, and Changing Data Types**
   - Subsetting Basics
   - Coercion in R
10. **Sorting Functions in R**
    - Sort and Order Functions
    - Max and Which.max Functions
    - Rank Function
11. **Vector Arithmetic in R**
    - Rescaling a Vector

- Operations with Two Vectors

12. **Indexes and Logical Vectors in R**
    - Indexing Basics
    - Logical Vectors
    - Using Which, Match, and %in%
13. **Tidyverse Package**
    - Filter Function
    - Pipes
    - Creating Data Frames
14. **Basic Plots in R**
    - Using the Hist Function
    - Creating Box Plots
    - Visualizing Images
15. **Summarizing Data**
    - Using Summarize Function
    - Multiple Summaries
    - Grouping and Arranging Data
16. **Sorting Data Frames**
    - Nested Sorting
    - Using Top_n
17. **Modifying Data Frames**
    - Adding or Changing Columns
    - Subsetting with Data.Table
    - Sorting Data Tables
18. **Control Flow in R**
    - Conditional Expressions
    - Defining Functions
    - For-Loops

Chapter 1: Introduction to R

Why R? What Is It Specifically Created For?

Imagine entering a high-stakes lab where scientists, analysts, and data wizards wield tools as powerful as their minds. In the arsenal is R—a programming language born specifically for the wild world of data analysis and statistical computing. R is like that quirky genius friend who's great in their field. It was invented early in the 90s by Ross Ihaka and Robert Gentleman as another programming language, but this one was meant to attack the problems presented by complex data where other languages failed.

R's true magic lies in how it makes statistical analysis easier. Ever tried handling gigantic datasets that look ready to swallow you whole? Or trying to make numbers tell a story so clearly even your grandma could get it? R is built to handle that mess beautifully, and it thrives where most general-purpose languages would sweat.

Why Choose R?

1. **Tailored to statistics and data analysis**: Unlike other languages, which are jack-of-all-trades, R was made for people crunching data, digging in for insights, and trying to get results that aren't just accurate but meaningful. Think of R as the Michelangelo of data analysis, sculpting raw data into beautiful, clear insights.
2. **Built-In Libraries & Packages Galore**: R comes with packages that are like powerful data potions. Need to do something super-specific, like analyze gene expression data? Or create gorgeous visualizations? R has a package for that. There are thousands of packages developed by the R community, so you're never far from a quick solution to your problem.
3. **Visualization Powers**: R spits out mere numbers, but instead, it transforms data into breathtaking visuals. Libraries such as `ggplot2`, mean your data might look like something taken straight out of an art gallery. Data visualization in R is not just making something look pretty; it is turning complicated information digestible.
4. **Community of Data Fanatics**: One of the great things about R is that it has a great community. Analysts, researchers, and statisticians in all parts of the world share packages, advice, and tools. So, if you are ever in a jam, you have a whole global squad ready to help you out.

In a nutshell, R was designed to be the ultimate tool for statisticians and data analysts. It doesn't merely handle data-it comprehends it, shapes it, and lets you narrate the story behind the numbers. And that, my dear, is why R is your best friend in data analysis!

Packages Installation in R

Good job! You have R going at this point, and that's great! But on its own, R is more like a starter toolkit-highly useful but ultimately, we want some high-powered tools to really help us get things done, right? That's where **packages** come in! These are collections of functions, data, and code that make R even more powerful. Want to make killer graphs? Handle complex stats? There's a package for almost anything you can imagine.

Why Install Packages?

Think of R as a blank canvas. Packages are the fancy brushes and paints that let you paint a masterpiece. Without packages, you are limited to R's basic functions. With packages, you are able to unlock advanced functionalities that can save you the time and headache of already created solutions by experts.

Installing Packages 101

Installing packages in R is super simple. Just use the `install.packages()` function, and R will handle the rest, pulling in all the code you need directly from CRAN (Comprehensive R Archive Network) or other repositories.

Here's how it goes:

Code for Installing a Package

Let's say you want to install the package `ggplot2`, a popular package for data visualization. Here's what you do:

```r
install.packages("ggplot2")
```

Step-by-Step Breakdown

1. **Type the Command**: `install.packages("ggplot2")`
2. **Hit Enter**: R will connect to CRAN (like a giant library of R packages) and pull in the `ggplot2` package files.

3. **Wait for the Installation to Complete**: R will show you some progress, downloading and installing the package.
4. **Load the Package**: Once installed, you need to load it into your R session using the `library()` function.

   ```r
   library(ggplot2)
   ```
5. **Use Your New Tool!**: Now `ggplot2` is ready to make your data visuals look gorgeous!

Want More Packages? Stack Them Up!

You can install multiple packages at once if you're feeling ambitious:

```r
install.packages(c("dplyr", "tidyr", "shiny"))
```

Here, you're bringing in `dplyr` for data wrangling, `tidyr` for cleaning data, and `shiny` to make interactive web applications. That's like getting yourself a super-charged data analysis toolkit in one go.

Pro Tip: Updating Packages

Packages get updated regularly, and to make sure you have the latest features, you can use this command:

```r
update.packages()
```

This checks all the packages you've installed and updates them if there are any new versions. Easy-peasy!

The Basics of R

Objects in R: The Building Blocks of Data Magic

Everything in R is an object. When you assign a value, a dataset, or a function, you are creating an object. Objects are containers holding a value or data you would like to work with. You can put a number in an object, store a bunch of text, or even a whole dataset.

Here's a super simple example:

```r
my_object <- 42
```

Here, `my_object` is an object that holds the value `42`. Now whenever you want to use that value, you just call `my_object`.

Variables: The Names for Your Objects

In R, **variables** are just names you give to your objects. They're labels that make it easy to keep track of the data you're storing.

Important Tip: Use `<-` to assign values to variables. Sure, `=` works too, but `<-` is the R way!

Example:

```r
name <- "Eman"
age <- 16
favorite_number <- 7
```

Now, `name`, `age`, and `favorite_number` are all variables holding different data. Try printing them in the console:

```r
print(name)
```

```r
print(age)
print(favorite_number)
```

Why <-?

`<-` is like an arrow pointing to where you're putting your data. It's quirky, but once you get used to it, it's like a secret handshake with R.

Functions: The Magic Wands of R

Functions are kind of little machines, which accept input, do something to it and give you output. R comes preloaded with lots of functions so you don't have to build everything from scratch each time. You call a function by writing its name and putting your input (known as arguments) in parentheses.

Here's an example:

```r
# Basic math function
result <- sum(10, 5, 3)
print(result)   # This will print 18
```

Or let's say you want to make everything in a word uppercase:

```r
shout <- toupper("hello world")
print(shout)   # Outputs: "HELLO WORLD"
```

Want to make your own function? Here's how:

```r
add_numbers <- function(a, b) {
  result <- a + b
  return(result)
}

print(add_numbers(3, 7))   # Outputs: 10
```

Here, `add_numbers` is your own function that takes two numbers, adds them, and returns the result. R functions can be as simple or as complex as you want.

Pre-Built Objects: R's Little Helpers

R comes with some **pre-built objects** that can save you tons of time. Let's take a look at a couple of them:

LETTERS: This is a built-in object that contains the uppercase English alphabet.
```r
print(LETTERS)
# Outputs: "A" "B" "C" ... "Z"
```

pi: Holds the value of π (pi), perfect for any math magic.
```r
Copy code
print(pi)
# Outputs: 3.141593
```

Want to randomly pick a letter? R's got your back:
```r
sample(LETTERS, 1)
# Outputs a random letter like "G" or "Q"
```

Basic Arithmetic Operations with Objects and Variables

R isn't just about fancy functions and built-in tools; you can use it for everyday math too!

```r
x <- 5
y <- 3

# Add
add <- x + y    # Outputs: 8

# Subtract
subtract <- x - y    # Outputs: 2
```

```r
# Multiply
multiply <- x * y     # Outputs: 15

# Divide
divide <- x / y       # Outputs: 1.666667

print(add)
print(subtract)
print(multiply)
print(divide)
```

Boom! Just like that, you're doing math in R.

Summary: The Key Takeaways

- **Objects**: Containers that hold data or values.
- **Variables**: Names you assign to objects.
- **Functions**: Pre-built or custom-made mini-programs that process data.
- **Pre-Built Objects**: R has some shortcuts like `LETTERS` and `pi` that are always ready for use.

Rules for Naming Variables in R

Naming your variables is like choosing names for your characters in a story; it matters, and there are some rules to follow so that R doesn't throw a fit.

1. Start with a Letter

- Your variable name **must start with a letter**, not a number or special character. So `age` and `myData` are good, but `1age` or `#value` won't work.

```r
# Correct
age <- 25

# Incorrect
1age <- 25    # This will throw an error
```

2. Use Letters, Numbers, or Dots/Underscores

- You can use **letters**, **numbers**, **dots** (`.`), and **underscores** (`_`). Just keep it readable!

```r
user_age <- 30
data.value <- 99
```

3. Case-Sensitive (Watch Out!)

- R is **case-sensitive**, meaning `Age` and `age` are two different variables.

```r
age <- 20
Age <- 25

# These are two separate variables
print(age)   # Outputs: 20
print(Age)   # Outputs: 25
```

4. No Spaces Allowed

- No spaces in variable names! If you need separation, use **underscores** or **camelCase** (starting each new word with a capital).

```r
# Correct
my_age <- 18
myAge <- 18

# Incorrect
my age <- 18   # This will throw an error
```

5. Avoid Reserved Words

- R has certain keywords it uses, like `if`, `else`, `for`, `TRUE`, `FALSE`, etc. Don't use these as variable names, or R will get all confused.

```r
# Avoid this
TRUE <- "yes"    # This will throw an error because TRUE is reserved
```

Commenting Your Code: Making it Human-Friendly

Programming without comments is like writing a book without chapters or any punctuation in it—it is a mess! Comments are your way of explaining what your code does, why you did it, or how it works.

How to Comment in R

In R, comments start with the # symbol. Anything written after # on the same line is ignored by R.

Comment Examples

1. Single-Line Comments

Use comments to label sections or explain individual lines:

r

```r
# This variable stores the user's age
age <- 25

# Adding 5 to the age
new_age <- age + 5
```

2. Multi-Line Comments

If you need to explain something more complex, you can use multiple single-line comments in a row:

r
```r
# Function to calculate the area of a circle
# Takes radius as an argument
# Returns the calculated area
calculate_area <- function(radius) {
  area <- pi * radius^2   # Area formula
  return(area)
}
```

3. Inline Comments

You can add comments on the same line as code if it's something quick:

r
```r
total_price <- 100 * 1.05   # Adding 5% tax
```

Commenting Tips

- **Explain the Why**: Sometimes it's more useful to explain *why* you're doing something rather than *how* (code often explains the "how" itself).
- **Be Brief but Clear**: Don't go overboard. Comments should be helpful but not cluttered.

Example: Putting It All Together

Here's a little code snippet with well-named variables and comments. This calculates the final price of an item after tax and a discount:

```r
# Defining the item price
item_price <- 250   # Price in dollars

# Tax rate as a decimal (10% tax)
tax_rate <- 0.10

# Discount rate as a decimal (15% discount)
discount_rate <- 0.15

# Calculate the price after tax
price_after_tax <- item_price * (1 + tax_rate)   # Adding tax

# Apply discount
final_price <- price_after_tax * (1 - discount_rate)   # Applying discount

# Print the final price
print(final_price)   # Outputs the price after tax and discount
```

With comments like these, anyone who reads your code can understand the purpose of each step.

In Summary:

- Follow naming rules to keep variables error-free and readable.
- Use comments to add clarity and context to your code.

Data Types in R

Data in R varies. Each data type informs R how it should handle the information. It is like giving R a heads-up about what it's working with: whether that is just numbers, text, or perhaps something entirely different.

Let's go through the main types, with fun examples and code for each!

a. Numeric

- For all things number-related (decimals, whole numbers).
- Example: Age, prices, measurements.

```r
# Numeric examples
age <- 16        # Whole number
price <- 99.99   # Decimal
```

b. Integer

- Special type for whole numbers. Add an `L` after a number to mark it as an integer.
- Use this when you're working with counts or discrete values.

```r
# Integer example
days_in_week <- 7L
```

c. Character (Strings)

- For text data. Think of names, addresses, or any non-numeric information.
- Text is always wrapped in quotes (" ").

```r
# Character examples
name <- "Xenia"
favorite_food <- "Pizza"
```

d. Logical (Boolean)

- For TRUE or FALSE values. Great for anything that's either/or, like on/off or yes/no questions.

```r
# Logical example
is_student <- TRUE
is_tired <- FALSE
```

e. Factor

- Special data type for categories. This is super useful for data with fixed options, like "Yes", "No", "Maybe".
- Think of it as assigning levels to values.

```r
# Factor example
color <- factor("blue", levels = c("red", "blue", "green"))
```

f. Complex

- For complex numbers with real and imaginary parts. Rarely used but good to know if you're dealing with advanced math.

```r
# Complex example
complex_num <- 3 + 2i
```

Example: Identifying Data Types

You can check the type of any data in R with `class()`:

```r
print(class(age))          # Outputs: "numeric"
print(class(name))         # Outputs: "character"
print(class(is_student))   # Outputs: "logical"
```

Data Frames: The Heart and Soul of R

Alright, data frames are *the thing* in R. Think of a **data frame** as a super-organized table where you store all your data in a structured way—perfect for analysis!

What's a Data Frame?

Imagine a spreadsheet where each **column** is a variable (like age, name, or favorite_food), and each **row** is an observation (like a single person's data). Data frames make it easy to manage data in R and are the backbone of many R projects.

How to Create a Data Frame

You can create data frames using the data.frame() function. Here's an example with a little character lineup:

```r
# Create a data frame of people and their characteristics
friends <- data.frame(
  name = c("Xenia", "Miya", "Amy", "Princess"),
  age = c(16, 17, 16, 18),
  favorite_food = c("Pizza", "Shawarma", "Chinese Rice", "Birthday Cake"),
  is_student = c(TRUE, TRUE, TRUE, FALSE)
)

# Print the data frame
print(friends)
```

This code creates a data frame called friends with four columns: name, age, favorite_food, and is_student.

Accessing Data in a Data Frame

Once you have a data frame, you can grab specific rows, columns, or even individual values.

Accessing Columns

Use $ to access a specific column:

```r
print(friends$name)   # Outputs: "Xenia" "Miya" "Amy" "Princess"
print(friends$age)    # Outputs: 16 17 16 18
```

Accessing Rows and Specific Values

You can also use [,] with row and column indices to be extra specific. Format: data_frame[row, column]

```r
# Get the first row, all columns
print(friends[1, ])

# Get the first row, first column
print(friends[1, 1])

# Get all rows of the 'favorite_food' column
print(friends[, "favorite_food"])
```

Adding and Removing Columns in a Data Frame

You can add new columns to your data frame easily:

```r
# Add a new column 'hobby'
friends$hobby <- c("Reading", "Violin", "Singing", "Coding")
print(friends)  # New column added with hobbies
```

To remove a column, use NULL:

```r
# Remove the 'hobby' column
friends$hobby <- NULL
print(friends)  # Column 'hobby' is now removed
```

Summary: Data Types and Data Frames

- **Data Types**: R recognizes types like numeric, integer, character, logical, and factor, each with its unique purpose.
- **Data Frames**: Organized tables that let you work with multiple variables and observations efficiently.

Examining an Object in R

R comes with some really neat functions to inspect our objects. You can find out the type of data, look inside to see the structure, and even grab specific pieces you want to work with. We'll look at two powerful tools to help you do this: the $ **accessor** and the `class()` function.

---

1. The $ Accessor: Your Go-To for Columns

The $ symbol is like R's VIP pass for accessing specific columns in data frames. It lets you quickly and easily pull out any column you want to work with from your data frame.

Let's say you've got a data frame of your friends and their favorite foods (again—because it's a solid example, alright?):

```r
# Data frame of friends
friends <- data.frame(
  name = c("Xenia", "Miya", "Amy", "Princess"),
  age = c(16, 17, 16, 18),
  favorite_food = c("Pizza", "Shawarma", "Chinese Rice", "Birthday Cake")
)

# Print the data frame to see it
print(friends)
```

Now, let's use $ to grab just the `name` column:

```r
# Use $ to access the 'name' column
print(friends$name)   # Outputs: "Xenia" "Miya" "Amy" "Princess"
```

The $ accessor is super handy because you don't need to deal with indices; you simply tell R which column you want by its name. It's quick, easy, and oh-so-satisfying.

You can also use $ to modify a column or even add a new one:

r
```
# Adding a new column with $ accessor
friends$is_student <- c(TRUE, TRUE, TRUE, FALSE)
print(friends)  # Now includes the 'is_student' column
```

2. The `class()` Function: Discover Your Object's Identity

Ever wondered, "What *type* of data am I working with here?" The `class()` function has the answer! It's like asking R, "Hey, what's this thing I'm looking at?"

Here's how you can use `class()`:

r
```
# Check the class of the entire 'friends' data frame
print(class(friends))  # Outputs: "data.frame"

# Check the class of a specific column
print(class(friends$age))   # Outputs: "numeric"
print(class(friends$name))  # Outputs: "character"
```

This comes in handy when you're trying to apply functions or transformations and want to make sure they're compatible with your data type.

Let's make it interesting by adding a factor column to `friends` and checking its class:

r
```
# Add a new column with factor data type
friends$color <- factor(c("Blue", "Red", "Green", "Blue"))

# Check the class of the new column
print(class(friends$color))  # Outputs: "factor"
```

This way, `class()` helps you identify the object type, so you know exactly what you're dealing with.

Examining Your Data Like a Pro

These two tools are just the beginning. Here are some pro tips to get even more out of them:

Combining $ with functions: You can use $ along with functions like `mean()`, `sum()`, or `length()` to get quick insights about specific columns.

```r
# Get the average age
mean_age <- mean(friends$age)
print(mean_age)   # Outputs: 16.75
```

- **Double-checking with `class()`**: Whenever you're unsure, run `class()` on the object, and it'll save you a ton of trial-and-error.

By getting familiar with $ and `class()`, you're building the foundation to examine and manipulate data with precision and confidence. Keep playing around, and soon you'll be examining objects in R like the boss you are!

Factors, Lists, and Matrices in R

Factors:

Factors are R's way of handling *categorical* data (data that fits into a limited set of categories). Let's say you're categorizing your friends based on Hogwarts Houses —a classic use for factors.

Here's how you might use factors:

```r
# A vector of Hogwarts Houses
houses <- c("Gryffindor", "Slytherin", "Ravenclaw", "Gryffindor", "Hufflepuff")

# Convert to a factor
house_factor <- factor(houses)

# Print the factor
print(house_factor)
# [1] Gryffindor Slytherin Ravenclaw Gryffindor Hufflepuff
# Levels: Gryffindor Hufflepuff Ravenclaw Slytherin
```

When you convert houses into a factor, R automatically detects the unique categories (called *levels*), and it organizes your data accordingly.

Setting Factor Levels

Want to control the order of the levels? Let's say you're feeling particularly loyal to Hufflepuff, so you want it to be first:

```r
# Re-order factor levels
house_factor <- factor(houses, levels = c("Hufflepuff", "Gryffindor", "Ravenclaw", "Slytherin"))

print(house_factor)
```

Now, `Hufflepuff` will appear first among the levels. This can be helpful when plotting or analyzing data, as the order of levels can impact the results.

Lists:

Lists are like R's goody bags. You can put *anything* in a list: numbers, strings, data frames, even other lists. If your project feels a bit chaotic, a list can keep everything organized.

Here's an example list that stores data about you and your besties:

```r
# Create a list
friends_info <- list(
  names = c("Xenia", "Miya", "Amy", "Princess"),
  ages = c(16, 17, 16, 18),
  houses = house_factor,  # Using our factor from above
  favorite_foods = c("Pizza", "Shawarma", "Chinese Rice", "Birthday Cake")
)

# Print the list
print(friends_info)
```

Each element in `friends_info` is accessible by name or by position. Let's pull out some details:

```r
# Accessing by name
print(friends_info$names)   # Outputs: "Xenia" "Miya" "Amy" "Princess"

# Accessing by position
print(friends_info[[2]])   # Outputs: 16 17 16 18
```

You can even nest lists inside lists (aka "listception") if your data is super complex. Lists are endlessly flexible and can handle all kinds of wild data combos.

Matrices:

Matrices are two-dimensional data structures where all elements must be the same type (numeric, character, etc.). Imagine a classroom seating chart with rows and columns; matrices are perfect for that kind of data.

Creating a Basic Matrix

Let's set up a matrix to show scores on three exams for four students:

```r
# Exam scores matrix
exam_scores <- matrix(
  c(85, 90, 78, 88, 92, 85, 79, 81, 95, 89, 87, 93),
  nrow = 4,
  ncol = 3,
  byrow = TRUE
)

# Print the matrix
print(exam_scores)
```

This will give you:

```css
     [,1] [,2] [,3]
[1,]  85   90   78
[2,]  88   92   85
[3,]  79   81   95
[4,]  89   87   93
```

Each row is a student, and each column is an exam score. You can access individual elements, rows, or columns:

```r
# Access the score of the 2nd student on the 3rd exam
print(exam_scores[2, 3])   # Outputs: 85

# Access all scores of the 1st student
print(exam_scores[1, ])    # Outputs: 85 90 78
```

```r
# Access all scores on the 2nd exam
print(exam_scores[, 2])   # Outputs: 90 92 81 87
```

Naming Rows and Columns

Let's make it clear who's who by adding some names:

r
```
# Add row and column names
rownames(exam_scores) <- c("Xenia", "Miya", "Amy", "Princess")
colnames(exam_scores) <- c("Exam 1", "Exam 2", "Exam 3")

print(exam_scores)
```

Now your matrix will look like this:

markdown
```
         Exam 1 Exam 2 Exam 3
Xenia       85     90     78
Miya        88     92     85
Amy         79     81     95
Princess    89     87     93
```

Combining Matrices

Got two matrices you want to combine? R's got you covered with `cbind()` (for columns) and `rbind()` (for rows). Let's add a new exam score:

r
```
# New exam scores for Exam 4
exam4 <- c(86, 91, 88, 90)

# Add it as a new column
exam_scores <- cbind(exam_scores, "Exam 4" = exam4)

print(exam_scores)
```

Now you've got all four exams in one matrix—easy peasy.

Summing Up the Trio of Data Types

- **Factors**: Perfect for categories. They keep data organized and allow you to set custom levels.
- **Lists**: The Swiss army knife of data containers, capable of holding anything and everything.
- **Matrices**: Ideal for 2D data of the same type, with easy row/column manipulation.

With these tools, you're ready to tackle data in R like a pro! Whether it's organizing, categorizing, or stacking data, these data types have your back.

Vectors in R

Think of vectors as R's favorite way to store a bunch of values all in one spot. Want to keep track of the scores from a game night? That's a vector!

Creating a Vector

There are tons of ways to create vectors, but here's a classic one using the `c()` function:

```r
# Scores from game night
scores <- c(80, 92, 77, 85, 90)
print(scores)
# [1] 80 92 77 85 90
```

Here, `scores` is a **numeric vector** that stores our game night results. You can create vectors with any data type, like characters or logical values.

```r
# A character vector for team names
teams <- c("Wolves", "Dragons", "Phoenix", "Tigers")
print(teams)
# [1] "Wolves" "Dragons" "Phoenix" "Tigers"
```

Naming Vectors:

Names make vectors *fancy* and easier to read! Let's assign names to each game night score so we know who got what.

```r
# Naming the scores vector
names(scores) <- c("Player 1", "Player 2", "Player 3", "Player 4", "Player 5")
print(scores)
# Player 1 Player 2 Player 3 Player 4 Player 5
#       80       92       77       85       90
```

Now each score is labeled with the player's name—way easier to tell who got what! And if you want to get, say, Player 3's score, you can just call it by name:

r
```
# Accessing by name
print(scores["Player 3"]) # Output: 77
```

Sequence Function

The `seq()` function is R's shortcut for creating a series of numbers. Need a sequence from 1 to 10? Done! Do you Need every other number between 1 and 20? Easy!

r
```
# Sequence from 1 to 10
seq_1_to_10 <- seq(1, 10)
print(seq_1_to_10)
# [1]  1  2  3  4  5  6  7  8  9 10
```

Want to get a little bit fancy? Use `by` to control the intervals.

r
```
# Sequence from 1 to 20, counting by 2
seq_by_2 <- seq(1, 20, by = 2)
print(seq_by_2)
# [1]  1  3  5  7  9 11 13 15 17 19
```

Or, maybe you want a sequence with a specific length? Use `length.out`.

r
```
# Sequence from 1 to 10 with 5 values
seq_length <- seq(1, 10, length.out = 5)
print(seq_length)
# [1]  1.0  3.2  5.5  7.8 10.0
```

A Mini Challenge with seq():

Let's create a countdown from 10 to 1. Think of it as a R-powered launch

```r
# Countdown from 10 to 1
countdown <- seq(10, 1, by = -1)
print(countdown)
#  [1] 10  9  8  7  6  5  4  3  2  1
```

Combining Vectors

Got multiple vectors you want to stack? Use `c()` to join them together.

```r
# Game night scores, round 2
scores_round2 <- c(82, 91, 79, 88, 95)

# Combining scores from both rounds
all_scores <- c(scores, scores_round2)
print(all_scores)
# Player 1 Player 2 Player 3 Player 4 Player 5
#       80       92       77       85       90
# Player 1 Player 2 Player 3 Player 4 Player 5
#       82       91       79       88       95
```

Summary

Vectors are *powerful*, flexible, and super customizable. They allow you to build vectors by hand, name every element, or create automatic sequences. Vectors give you the flexibility to store, label, and manipulate data like a pro while keeping your data beautifully organized and ready for any analysis.

Subsetting, Coercion and Changing Data Types

Subsetting in R:

Subsetting is like handpicking the best ingredients for your recipe. Whether you need a single value, a slice, or a specific chunk, R's got you covered!

Subsetting with Indices

This is the simplest way. Just tell R which positions you want, and voilà!

```r
# Our trusty vector of game night scores
scores <- c(80, 92, 77, 85, 90)

# Getting the score of the 2nd player
print(scores[2])   # Output: 92

# Getting the scores of the 2nd to 4th players
print(scores[2:4])   # Output: 92 77 85
```

Subsetting with Logical Values

Need to filter out scores over 80? Logical values to the rescue!

```r
# Scores greater than 80
high_scores <- scores[scores > 80]
print(high_scores)   # Output: 92 85 90
```

Subsetting with Names

If you've named your elements, use those labels!

```r
# Naming the scores
```

```r
names(scores) <- c("Alice", "Bob", "Charlie", "Dana", "Eve")

# Get Dana's score
print(scores["Dana"])   # Output: 85
```

Coercion in R:

Coercion is R's polite way of saying, "I think this should all be the same type, so I'll help by converting it." Sometimes, R automatically coerces types, especially in vectors; sometimes, you have to nudge it along.

Automatic Coercion: R's Auto-Pilot

If you mix types in a vector, R will automatically try to coerce everything to the most flexible type (usually `character`). Check this out:

```r
# Mixing numbers and characters
mixed_vector <- c(42, "Data", 78)
print(mixed_vector)   # Output: "42" "Data" "78"
# Notice how R turned the numbers into characters to keep it uniform!
```

Manual Coercion: Taking Control

Let's say you've got numbers saved as characters (maybe they came from a text file), and you want to treat them as actual numbers. Enter `as.numeric()`, `as.character()`, etc.

```r
# Character vector that looks numeric
char_numbers <- c("5", "10", "15")

# Converting to numeric
numeric_numbers <- as.numeric(char_numbers)
print(numeric_numbers)   # Output: 5 10 15
```

Changing Data Types:

Sometimes R needs a little more guidance to transform data the way you want. Luckily, you have `as.numeric()`, `as.character()`, and friends to turn any object into the right type.

From Logical to Numeric

Logicals (TRUE/FALSE) are often used as 1/0. Converting them can make things a lot easier for calculations.

```r
# Logical vector
pass_fail <- c(TRUE, FALSE, TRUE)

# Convert to numeric
numeric_pass_fail <- as.numeric(pass_fail)
print(numeric_pass_fail)  # Output: 1 0 1
```

Converting Data Frames Columns

Say you've got a data frame, and one of the columns is character-based when you need it to be numeric. You can convert that column on the spot.

```r
# Sample data frame
df <- data.frame(
  name = c("Alice", "Bob", "Charlie"),
  score = c("90", "88", "85")  # Notice: score is character
)

# Convert score to numeric
df$score <- as.numeric(df$score)
print(df)
#      name score
# 1   Alice    90
# 2     Bob    88
# 3 Charlie    85
```

Beware of NAs: If you try to convert non-numeric strings, R will return NA as a way of saying, "This doesn't make sense."

```r
# Converting non-numeric character to numeric
mixed_chars <- c("42", "hello", "100")
num_chars <- as.numeric(mixed_chars)
print(num_chars)
# Output: 42 NA 100
```

Summary

There you go! You now wield the power of subsetting, coercion, and type conversions in R like a true data wizard.

Sorting Functions in R

Sorting and Ordering in R:

Sorting with the `sort()` Function

Imagine you have a messy array of numbers, and you want to put them in order. The `sort()` function is your trusty sidekick for this job!

```r
# Our unsorted scores
scores <- c(90, 70, 85, 95, 80)

# Sorting in ascending order
sorted_scores <- sort(scores)
print(sorted_scores)   # Output: 70 80 85 90 95
```

Sorting in Descending Order

Want to flip the script and sort from high to low? Just add the `decreasing = TRUE` argument.

```r
# Sorting in descending order
sorted_scores_desc <- sort(scores, decreasing = TRUE)
print(sorted_scores_desc)   # Output: 95 90 85 80 70
```

Using `order()` to Get Indices

If you want to know the order of indices instead of the sorted values, `order()` comes to the rescue!

```r
# Getting the order of indices
ordered_indices <- order(scores)
print(ordered_indices)   # Output: 2 5 3 1 4 (which means scores[2] is the smallest)
```

And you can use this to rearrange your original vector:

```r
# Rearranging using ordered indices
scores_sorted_by_indices <- scores[ordered_indices]
print(scores_sorted_by_indices)  # Output: 70 80 85 90 95
```

Finding the Maximum Value: `max()` and `which.max()` Functions

Using `max()` to Find the Highest Score

The `max()` function is your go-to for finding the peak of the mountain.

```r
# Getting the maximum score
highest_score <- max(scores)
print(highest_score)  # Output: 95
```

Using `which.max()` to Find the Index of the Maximum Value

Need to know who scored that highest score? Use `which.max()`, and it'll point you right to the culprit!

```r
# Finding the index of the maximum score
max_index <- which.max(scores)
print(max_index)  # Output: 4 (the position of the highest score)
```

Now, let's see who scored that!

```r
# Who got the highest score?
print(paste("The highest score was by:", names(scores[max_index])))  # If names were assigned
```

Ranking with the `rank()` Function

Ranking is like giving each score a shiny medal. Let's see how to do this!

Basic Ranking

The `rank()` function assigns ranks to the values in your vector. Ties are given average ranks.

```r
# Assigning ranks
ranked_scores <- rank(scores)
print(ranked_scores)  # Output: 2 1 3.5 5 4 (where the smallest score gets rank 1)
```

Dealing with Ties

If there are ties, they will be averaged. Let's add some duplicates for fun!

```r
# Adding some ties
new_scores <- c(90, 70, 85, 95, 85)

# Ranking with ties
ranked_new_scores <- rank(new_scores)
print(ranked_new_scores)  # Output: 3 1 2.5 5 2.5 (85 shares the average rank of 2.5)
```

Ranking in Descending Order

Want to rank from highest to lowest? Just add the `ties.method` parameter.

```r
# Ranking in descending order
ranked_new_scores_desc <- rank(new_scores, ties.method = "first", na.last = "keep")
print(ranked_new_scores_desc)  # Output: 4 1 3 5 3 (first occurrence gets the rank)
```

Putting It All Together

And now, you have this powerful set of tools ready to go for sorting, finding maximum values, and ranking your data in R! You have now learned how to keep everything clean, well-organized, and in its proper place, just as organizing the closet. Now it's time to rule the kingdom of data!

Vector Arithmetic in R

Basic Operations

Vectors in R can be treated like lists of numbers you can perform operations on. Think of it like giving each element its own little math problem to solve!

Addition and Subtraction

Let's start with some basic arithmetic! You can add or subtract numbers from all elements of a vector with ease.

```r
# Create a vector of scores
scores <- c(10, 20, 30, 40)

# Adding 5 to each score
new_scores_add <- scores + 5
print(new_scores_add)   # Output: 15 25 35 45

# Subtracting 2 from each score
new_scores_sub <- scores - 2
print(new_scores_sub)   # Output: 8 18 28 38
```

Multiplication and Division

Multiplying or dividing every element in the vector is just as simple!

```r
# Multiplying each score by 2
doubled_scores <- scores * 2
print(doubled_scores)   # Output: 20 40 60 80

# Dividing each score by 10
divided_scores <- scores / 10
print(divided_scores)   # Output: 1 2 3 4
```

Element-wise Operations Between Two Vectors

You can also perform operations between two vectors of the same length!

```r
# Create another vector of adjustments
adjustments <- c(1, -1, 2, -2)

# Adding scores and adjustments together
final_scores <- scores + adjustments
print(final_scores)   # Output: 11 19 32 38
```

Rescaling a Vector in R:

Rescaling is like adjusting the size of your canvas. Maybe you want to make your scores fit within a certain range.

Rescaling Example

To rescale a vector to a new range (say between 0 and 1), you can use the formula:

$$\text{New Value} = \frac{x - \text{min}(x)}{\text{max}(x) - \text{min}(x)}$$

Let's see this in action!

```r
# Rescaling function
rescale <- function(x) {
  return ((x - min(x)) / (max(x) - min(x)))
}

# Rescaling our scores
rescaled_scores <- rescale(scores)
print(rescaled_scores)   # Output: 0.00 0.25 0.50 0.75 (normalized scores)
```

Rescaling to a New Range (a to b)

If you want to rescale to a new range, say from 5 to 10, use this formula:

New Value=a+((x−min(x))(max(x)−min(x))×(b−a))\text{New Value} = a + \left(\frac{(x - \text{min}(x))}{(\text{max}(x) - \text{min}(x))} \times (b - a) \right)New Value=a+((max(x)−min(x))(x−min(x))×(b−a))

Here's how you do it:

```r
# Rescale to a new range [5, 10]
rescale_to_range <- function(x, a, b) {
  return (a + (rescale(x) * (b - a)))
}

# Rescaling scores to be between 5 and 10
rescaled_range_scores <- rescale_to_range(scores, 5, 10)
print(rescaled_range_scores)   # Output: 5.0 6.25 7.5 8.75
```

Conclusion: Vector Math Is Magical!

Well, now you are all strong at adding, subtracting, multiplying and dividing vectors in R. You can even rescale your data as needed, too! Think of vectors as your trusty sidekicks, always ready for some arithmetic fun. Get ready to rock that data!

Indexes and Logical Vectors in R

Indexes in R:

Indexes in R are like treasure maps leading you to the elements of your vector or data frame. Each item has a special position—its index!

Using Indexes to Access Elements

Let's create a vector and see how indexing works!

```r
# Create a vector of fruits
fruits <- c("Apple", "Banana", "Cherry", "Date", "Elderberry")

# Accessing the first fruit
first_fruit <- fruits[1]
print(first_fruit)  # Output: "Apple"

# Accessing multiple fruits
selected_fruits <- fruits[c(2, 4)]
print(selected_fruits)  # Output: "Banana" "Date"
```

Negative Indexes

Negative indexing allows you to exclude certain elements.

```r
# Exclude the second fruit
excluded_fruit <- fruits[-2]
print(excluded_fruit)  # Output: "Apple" "Cherry" "Date" "Elderberry"
```

Logical Vectors in R:

Logical vectors are your trusty sidekicks when you want to filter, check conditions, or just have some fun with true/false values! They can hold values like TRUE, FALSE, or NA.

Creating Logical Vectors

Let's create a logical vector and see how it works.

```r
# Create a vector of numbers
numbers <- c(5, 10, 15, 20, 25)

# Create a logical vector for numbers greater than 15
logical_vector <- numbers > 15
print(logical_vector)  # Output: FALSE FALSE FALSE TRUE TRUE
```

Types of Logical Vectors

1. **Single Condition**: A vector with results of a single condition (like above).
2. **Multiple Conditions**: You can use & (and) and | (or) to combine conditions!

```r
# Logical vector for numbers greater than 10 AND less than 25
combined_logical <- numbers > 10 & numbers < 25
print(combined_logical)  # Output: FALSE TRUE TRUE TRUE FALSE
```

3. **Negation**: Use ! to reverse a logical vector.

```r
# Negating the previous logical vector
negated_logical <- !combined_logical
print(negated_logical)  # Output: TRUE FALSE FALSE FALSE TRUE
```

Using `which()`, `match()`, and `%in%`:

These functions help you find the positions or check membership in your vectors—like finding out who's on your guest list!

Using `which()`

The `which()` function returns the indices of the TRUE values in a logical vector.

```r
# Find positions of numbers greater than 15
positions <- which(numbers > 15)
print(positions)  # Output: 4 5
```

Using `match()`

`match()` finds the positions of matches of its first argument in its second argument.

```r
# Find where "Banana" and "Date" are in the fruits vector
match_positions <- match(c("Banana", "Date"), fruits)
print(match_positions)  # Output: 2 4
```

Using `%in%`

The `%in%` operator checks if elements of one vector are present in another.

```r
# Check which fruits are in the list
check_fruits <- c("Banana", "Cherry", "Fig")
present <- check_fruits %in% fruits
print(present)  # Output: TRUE TRUE FALSE
```

Putting It All Together!

Now you are well-equipped with a magical toolkit for using indexes, logical vectors, and membership functions in R. And when the wild of data is standing in front of you, don't get nervous with this map and compass! So, get out there and confidently start exploring the R landscape!

Tidyverse Package

Tidyverse:

The **tidyverse** is like a treasure box containing some very strong R data manipulation and visualization instruments. You can imagine this to be your toolkit like magic, that helps to do data in the clearest, most efficient fashion possible. First, installing and loading the tidyverse package:

Installing and Loading Tidyverse

r
```
# Install the tidyverse package (do this once)
install.packages("tidyverse")

# Load the tidyverse package
library(tidyverse)
```

Creating Data Frames:

Data frames are like tables in R, where you can store and manipulate data. They're structured in rows and columns, making them super easy to work with. Let's create one!

Creating a Data Frame

r
```
# Create a data frame of students
students <- data.frame(
  Name = c("Alice", "Bob", "Charlie", "Diana"),
  Age = c(20, 21, 22, 20),
  Score = c(85, 90, 78, 92)
)

# View the data frame
print(students)
```

Output:

  Name Age Score
1 Alice 20   85
2   Bob 21   90
3 Charlie 22   78
4 Diana 20   92
```

---

## The `filter()` Function:

The `filter()` function lets you pull out rows from your data frame based on specific conditions. It's like having a magic filter that only lets through the data you want!

### Using `filter()` to Get Specific Rows

```r
# Filter students who scored above 80
high_scorers <- students %>% filter(Score > 80)
print(high_scorers)
```

Output:

```markdown
  Name Age Score
1 Alice  20    85
2   Bob  21    90
3 Diana  20    92
```

Pipes: The Magic of Data Transformation!

Pipes (`%>%`) are like magic wands that let you string together multiple functions, making your code cleaner and more readable. Instead of nesting functions, you can pass the result of one function into the next!

Using Pipes with `filter()`

```r
# Using pipes to filter and select specific columns

```r
result <- students %>%
  filter(Score > 80) %>%
  select(Name, Score)

print(result)
```

Output:

markdown
```
  Name Score
1 Alice    85
2   Bob    90
3 Diana    92
```

A Fun Example: Combining Everything!

Let's combine our knowledge of data frames, filtering, and pipes to create an engaging example. Imagine we want to analyze students who are 20 years old and scored above 80!

r
```
# Filter and create a new data frame of specific students
young_high_scorers <- students %>%
  filter(Age == 20, Score > 80)

print(young_high_scorers)
```

Output:

```
  Name Age Score
1 Alice  20    85
2 Diana  20    92
```

Conclusion: Your Data Wizardry Journey Begins!

Now you're equipped with the tools of the tidyverse! You can create data frames, filter data, and use pipes to streamline your code. You've got the magic to manipulate data like a true wizard! So go forth and conjure up some amazing data insights!

Basic Plots in R

R has so many functions for plotting. Picture these plots as paintings that help you understand your data better. Let's start with a histogram, which is more or less like a bar chart showing how your data gets distributed!

The `hist()` Function:

The `hist()` function is perfect for creating histograms, allowing you to visualize the distribution of continuous data. Let's create a histogram using some randomly generated data.

Creating a Histogram with `hist()`

```r
# Generate some random data
set.seed(42)  # For reproducibility
data <- rnorm(1000, mean = 50, sd = 10)  # 1000 random values

# Create a histogram
hist(data,
     main = "Histogram of Random Data",  # Main title
     xlab = "Values",                    # X-axis label
     ylab = "Frequency",                 # Y-axis label
     col = "skyblue",                    # Fill color
     border = "black")                   # Border color
```

What You'll See:

You'll get a nice histogram showing the frequency of values. This helps you see how data is distributed around the mean (50).

What does a histogram looks like:

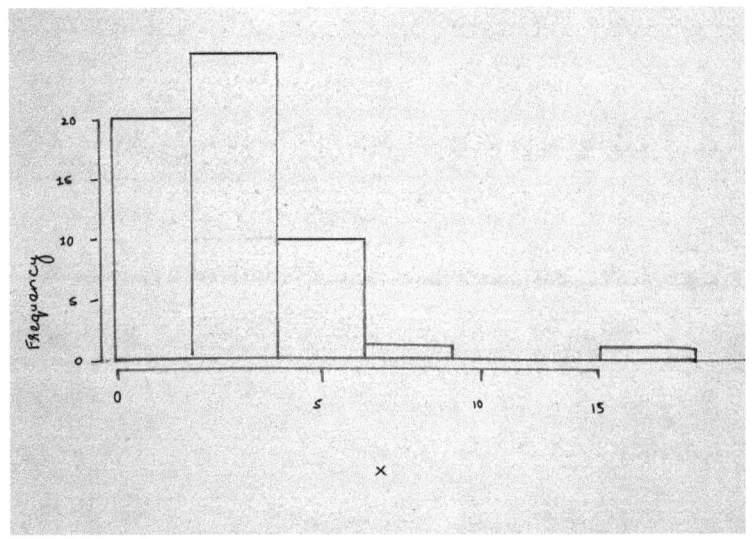

Box Plots:

Box plots are fantastic for visualizing the distribution of data through their quartiles. They show the median, upper, and lower quartiles, making them a quick way to see the spread and identify outliers.

Creating a Box Plot

Let's create a box plot using the same dataset.

r
```
# Create a box plot
boxplot(data,
        main = "Box Plot of Random Data",   # Main title
        ylab = "Values",                    # Y-axis label
        col = "lightgreen",                 # Fill color
        border = "darkgreen")               # Border color
```

```
# Adding a grid for better readability
grid()
```

What You'll See:

You'll get a box plot displaying the median, quartiles, and any outliers. It's a great way to see the spread of your data at a glance!

What a boxplot looks like:

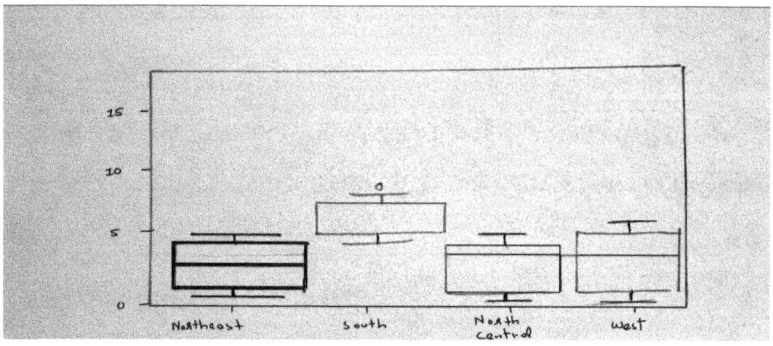

Displaying Images:

Sometimes, you want to display images in your R plots. For this, we can use the `rasterImage()` function. But first, let's load an image. Make sure you have an image saved in your working directory.

Example: Displaying an Image

r
```
# Load the necessary package for image handling
library(png)

# Load an image
img <- readPNG("path_to_your_image.png")  # Replace with your image path
```

```r
# Create a plot area
plot(1:2, type = "n", xlab = "", ylab = "", axes = FALSE)

# Display the image
rasterImage(img, 1, 1, 2, 2)  # Adjust the coordinates as needed
```

What You'll See:

You'll see your image displayed in the plot area! Adjust the coordinates in `rasterImage()` to fit your image properly in the plot area.

Putting It All Together: A Fun Data Visualization Journey!

Now you've got the tools to create histograms, box plots, and display images. Each of these visualizations helps convey different aspects of your data, making it easier to understand and communicate insights.

Final Example: Combining Plots!

Let's say we want to create both a histogram and a box plot in the same plot area.

```r
# Set up a 2x1 plot layout
par(mfrow = c(2, 1))

# Create histogram
hist(data,
     main = "Histogram of Random Data",
     xlab = "Values",
     ylab = "Frequency",
     col = "skyblue",
     border = "black")

# Create box plot
boxplot(data,
        main = "Box Plot of Random Data",
        ylab = "Values",
```

```
          col = "lightgreen",
          border = "darkgreen")

# Reset layout to default
par(mfrow = c(1, 1))
```

What You'll See:

You'll see both plots stacked vertically—what a beautiful data display!

Conclusion: Unleash Your Data Creativity!

Now you are ready to paint your data story with R! Histograms, box plots, and images are just the beginning of your visual journey. So grab your data, and let your creativity flow! Happy plotting!

Summarizing data

The `summarize()` Function:

The `summarize()` function allows you to condense your data into summary statistics. Think of it as creating a cheat sheet for your dataset!

Example: Summarizing a Dataset

Let's create a simple dataset to work with.

```r
# Load the dplyr package
library(dplyr)

# Create a sample data frame
data <- data.frame(
  group = c("A", "A", "B", "B", "C", "C"),
  values = c(10, 20, 30, 40, 50, 60)
)

# Summarize: Calculate the mean value for each group
summary_data <- data %>%
  group_by(group) %>%
  summarize(mean_value = mean(values))

print(summary_data)
```

What You'll See:

You'll get a summary table showing the mean value for each group—like getting the average score in a game!

Multiple Summaries: More Stats, More Fun!

Why settle for one summary when you can have many? You can calculate multiple summary statistics in one go!

Example: Multiple Summaries

r
```
# Summarize: Calculate mean, median, and total for each group
summary_multiple <- data %>%
  group_by(group) %>%
  summarize(
    mean_value = mean(values),
    median_value = median(values),
    total_value = sum(values)
  )

print(summary_multiple)
```

What You'll See:

This will give you a table with the mean, median, and total values for each group—super useful for understanding your data better!

The `pull()` Function: Extracting Data with Style!

The `pull()` function lets you extract a single column from a data frame as a vector. Think of it as grabbing a snack from the pantry—you just want a taste of one flavor!

Example: Using `pull()`

r
```
# Pull the 'mean_value' column
mean_values_vector <- summary_multiple %>%
  pull(mean_value)

print(mean_values_vector)
```

What You'll See:

You'll get a vector of mean values, making it easy to work with just that piece of data!

The `group_by()` Function:

The `group_by()` function is your best friend when you want to perform operations on subsets of data. It's like organizing your homework by subject—way easier to manage!

Example: Grouping Data

We've already used `group_by()` in previous examples, but let's see it in action again.

```r
# Group by 'group' and calculate total for each
grouped_data <- data %>%
  group_by(group) %>%
  summarize(total_value = sum(values))

print(grouped_data)
```

What You'll See:

A table showing the total value for each group—nice and organized!

The `arrange()` Function: Sorting Your Data for Clarity!

The `arrange()` function lets you sort your data in ascending or descending order. It's like tidying up your desk—everything in its right place!

Example: Sorting Data

```r
# Arrange the summary data in descending order by mean_value
sorted_data <- summary_multiple %>%
  arrange(desc(mean_value))

print(sorted_data)
```

What You'll See:

You'll see your summary data sorted from the highest mean value to the lowest—perfect for making quick comparisons!

Putting It All Together: A Fun Data Wrangling Adventure!

Now that you know how to summarize, group, pull, and arrange your data, you can tackle any dataset with confidence. Let's combine all these functions into one fun example.

Final Example: Full Data Workflow

```r
# Create a new data frame for a complete workflow
new_data <- data.frame(
  category = c("X", "X", "Y", "Y", "Z", "Z"),
  values = c(5, 15, 25, 35, 45, 55)
)

# Combine operations: group, summarize, arrange
final_summary <- new_data %>%
  group_by(category) %>%
  summarize(
    mean_value = mean(values),
    total_value = sum(values)
  ) %>%
  arrange(desc(mean_value))

# Pulling the mean values
mean_values_vector_final <- final_summary %>%
  pull(mean_value)

# Print results
print(final_summary)
print(mean_values_vector_final)
```

What You'll See:

You'll see a well-organized summary of means and totals sorted by category, along with a vector of mean values for easy access!

Conclusion: Your Data Wrangling Toolkit!

Congratulations! You have learned how to summarize, group, pull, and arrange your data in R. It is finally going to be possible to transform raw data into insightful summaries without much effort. Take your data and start playing around—you are on your way to becoming a data wizard!

Sorting Data Frames

The `arrange()` function from the **dplyr** package allows you to sort your data frame by one or more columns. You can sort in ascending or descending order, making it super flexible!

Example: Sorting a Data Frame

Let's create a simple data frame of students and their scores.

```r
# Load the dplyr package
library(dplyr)

# Create a sample data frame
students <- data.frame(
  name = c("Alice", "Bob", "Charlie", "David"),
  score = c(88, 95, 78, 85)
)

# Sort the data frame by score in ascending order
sorted_students <- students %>%
  arrange(score)

print(sorted_students)
```

What You'll See:

The output will be a nicely sorted list of students based on their scores, from lowest to highest.

Nested Sorting:

Sometimes, you need to sort by more than one column—like sorting by score and then by name. This is called nested sorting!

Example: Nested Sorting

Let's expand our dataset to include scores and ages.

```r
# Create a more detailed data frame
students <- data.frame(
  name = c("Alice", "Bob", "Charlie", "David", "Edward"),
  score = c(88, 95, 85, 85, 88),
  age = c(20, 22, 21, 22, 20)
)

# Nested sorting: first by score (descending), then by name
(ascending)
nested_sorted_students <- students %>%
  arrange(desc(score), name)

print(nested_sorted_students)
```

What You'll See:

You'll get a list of students sorted primarily by their scores (highest first), and in case of ties, sorted by name alphabetically. It's like being both the judge and the referee in a talent show!

Using `top_n()`: Getting the Top Entries

The `top_n()` function is fantastic for quickly grabbing the top entries from your data. It's like having a VIP pass to the best seats in the house!

Example: Using `top_n()`

Let's find the top three students by score.

```r
# Get the top 3 students by score
top_students <- students %>%
  top_n(3, score)

print(top_students)
```

What You'll See:

This will display the top three students based on their scores—ideal for identifying the stars of the class!

Combining It All: Sorting and Finding Top Entries

Let's put all our sorting skills together. We'll sort the students by score and then grab the top three scores.

Final Example: Sorting and Using `top_n()` Together

```r
# Sort the data frame and then get the top 3 students by score
final_top_students <- students %>%
  arrange(desc(score)) %>%
  top_n(3, score)

print(final_top_students)
```

What You'll See:

You'll get a list of the top three students with the highest scores, neatly arranged in descending order!

Conclusion: Your Sorting Superpowers!

Now that you know how to sort data frames, nested, and get top entries in R, you can sort student scores or any other data by using such functions. Start sorting like a pro; you are ready!

Modifying Data Frames

Adding or Changing Columns in `data.table`

In **data.table**, adding or modifying a column is a breeze! You can do it in one simple step, and it's almost like magic!

Example: Adding and Changing Columns

First, let's create a data table and see how to add and change columns.

```r
# Load the data.table package
library(data.table)

# Create a sample data table
students_dt <- data.table(
  name = c("Alice", "Bob", "Charlie"),
  score = c(88, 95, 78)
)

# Add a new column for age
students_dt[, age := c(20, 22, 21)]

# Change the score for Charlie
students_dt[name == "Charlie", score := 80]

print(students_dt)
```

What You'll See:

The output will show your data table with a new **age** column and Charlie's score updated to 80. It's like customizing your character in a video game!

Subsetting with `data.table`

Subsetting in **data.table** is incredibly efficient. You can easily filter rows based on conditions—like picking out your favorite candies from a mixed bag!

Example: Subsetting Data Tables

Let's say we want to find all students with scores above 85.

r
```
# Subset students with scores greater than 85
high_scorers <- students_dt[score > 85]

print(high_scorers)
```

What You'll See:

This will give you a data table with only the students who scored more than 85, making it easy to identify the top performers!

Sorting Data Tables

Sorting data tables is as easy as pie! You can sort by one or multiple columns just like sorting your favorite songs in a playlist.

Example: Sorting Data Tables

Let's sort our students based on their scores in descending order.

r
```
# Sort students by score in descending order
sorted_students_dt <- students_dt[order(-score)]

print(sorted_students_dt)
```

What You'll See:

The output will be a neatly sorted data table where the students with the highest scores are at the top, making it easy to see who's acing it!

Putting It All Together

Let's create a comprehensive example that combines adding columns, subsetting, and sorting.

Final Example: Full Workflow

```r
# Create a new data table
students_dt <- data.table(
  name = c("Alice", "Bob", "Charlie", "David", "Edward"),
  score = c(88, 95, 78, 85, 88)
)

# Add age column
students_dt[, age := c(20, 22, 21, 22, 20)]

# Change Bob's score
students_dt[name == "Bob", score := 97]

# Subset students with scores greater than or equal to 88
high_scorers <- students_dt[score >= 88]

# Sort high scorers by score in descending order
sorted_high_scorers <- high_scorers[order(-score)]

print(sorted_high_scorers)
```

What You'll See:

This will produce a final table of students who scored 88 or more, sorted from highest to lowest score. You'll feel like a data wizard!

Conclusion: Your Data.table Toolkit!

You have become a ninja at data manipulation because you can add or change columns, subset your data tables, and sort them in the most efficient way. Be it student scores or some other data, this package makes working with data smooth and swift. So go on, get into your data, and shine it up!

Control Flow in R

Conditional Expressions in R

Conditional expressions in R are like asking questions—if a certain condition is true, you do one thing; if it's false, you do another. Think of it as a traffic light: green means go, and red means stop!

Example: Using `if`, `else if`, and `else`

Let's write a simple program that checks a student's score and determines whether they passed or failed.

```r
# Define a score
score <- 85

# Check the score using conditional expressions
if (score >= 90) {
  result <- "Grade A: Excellent!"
} else if (score >= 75) {
  result <- "Grade B: Good Job!"
} else {
  result <- "Grade C: Needs Improvement."
}

print(result)
```

What You'll See:

If the score is 85, you'll get a response saying, "Grade B: Good Job!" It's like getting a report card straight from the teacher!

Defining Functions in R

Functions are reusable blocks of code that perform a specific task—think of them as magic spells that you can cast whenever you need!

Example: Creating a Function

Let's create a function that calculates the square of a number.

```r
# Define a function to calculate the square of a number
calculate_square <- function(x) {
  return(x^2)
}

# Call the function with different numbers
square_of_4 <- calculate_square(4)
square_of_10 <- calculate_square(10)

print(square_of_4)    # Output: 16
print(square_of_10)   # Output: 100
```

What You'll See:

When you call the function with 4 and 10, you'll get back 16 and 100, respectively! It's like having a calculator in your pocket!

For-Loops: Repeating Tasks Like a Pro

For-loops allow you to repeat actions multiple times, which is super handy for tasks like processing lists or data. It's like a DJ playing your favorite song on repeat!

Example: Using a For-Loop

Let's create a for-loop that prints the squares of the first five natural numbers.

```r
# For-loop to print squares of numbers from 1 to 5
for (i in 1:5) {
  square <- calculate_square(i)
  print(paste("The square of", i, "is", square))
}
```

What You'll See:

The output will be:

```csharp
[1] "The square of 1 is 1"
[1] "The square of 2 is 4"
[1] "The square of 3 is 9"
[1] "The square of 4 is 16"
[1] "The square of 5 is 25"
```

It's like a little motivational speech for each number—"You're amazing, keep it up!"

Putting It All Together

Let's create a comprehensive example that incorporates conditional expressions, functions, and for-loops.

Final Example: A Fun Program to Grade Students

```r
# Define a function to grade based on score
grade_student <- function(score) {
  if (score >= 90) {
    return("A: Excellent!")
  } else if (score >= 75) {
    return("B: Good Job!")
  } else {
    return("C: Needs Improvement.")
  }
}

# Scores of several students
student_scores <- c(95, 82, 67, 89, 74)

# For-loop to grade each student
for (score in student_scores) {
  result <- grade_student(score)
```

```
  print(paste("Score:", score, "| Result:", result))
}
```

What You'll See:

This program will print the scores along with their corresponding grades for each student. It's like holding a mini graduation ceremony for your data!

Conclusion: Your Programming Toolbox!

You now have a really powerful toolbox populated with conditional expressions, functions, and for-loops! These tools will empower you to write much smarter, effective R code.you might say, like a master chef preparing a perfect meal. Off you go. Experiment, find, and make your code work for you! Happy coding!

Conclusion

Moving ahead in our path into R, we have toured a wide landscape of foundational ideas, tools, and techniques that are essential for data analysis. From the basics of R, through talking about what this might mean and entail-and why it speaks especially strongly to this area and language in which so many statisticians and data scientists find their work represented and preferred-we have explored everything from installing packages to mastering data types and structures, learning how R's powerful capabilities can take us far beyond simple forms of data manipulation and visualization.

We discussed conditional expressions, presented the concept of defining a function for code reusability, and how we can automate repetitive code using for-loops. Each concept was accompanied with examples and snippets of code for better clarity and retention.

Thus, practice and experimentation are crucial as we continue our data analysis journey. With what you now know, you are well on your way to becoming an proficient R programmer when facing more complex data analysis challenges!

Sincerely,
Eman Ahmad

www.ingramcontent.com/pod-product-compliance
Lightning Source LLC
Chambersburg PA
CBHW070410230526
45471CB00006B/2728